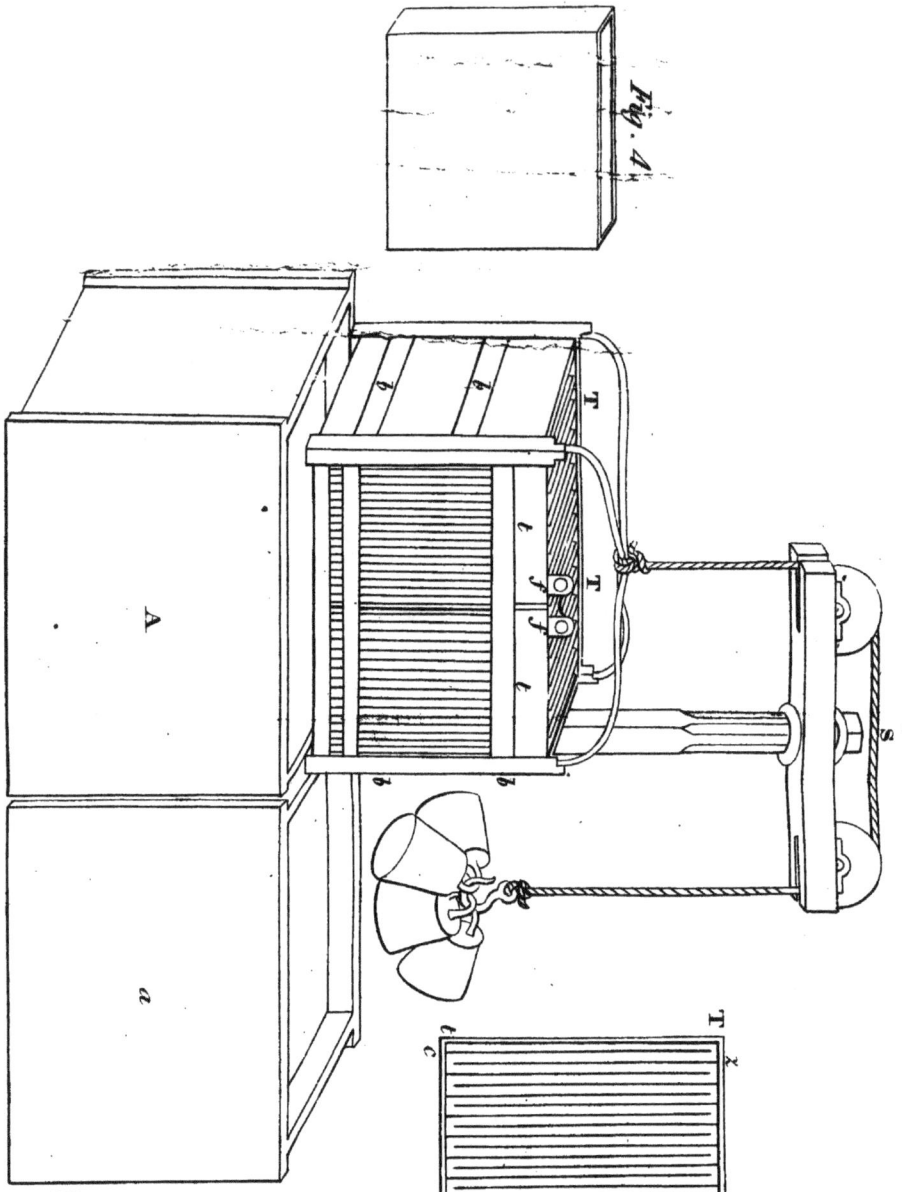

CALORIMOTOR.

Fig. 4.

Fig. 1.

Fig. 2.

Fig. 3.

Drawn & Engraved by Kneass, Young &c.

A NEW THEORY

OF

GALVANISM,

SUPPORTED BY SOME

EXPERIMENTS AND OBSERVATIONS

MADE BY MEANS OF THE

CALORIMOTOR,

A NEW GALVANIC INSTRUMENT.

ALSO,

A NEW MODE OF

DECOMPOSING POTASH

EXTEMPORANEOUSLY.

READ BEFORE THE ACADEMY OF NATURAL
SCIENCES, PHILADELPHIA.

BY ROBERT HARE, M. D.

PROFESSOR OF CHEMISTRY IN THE MEDICAL DEPARTMENT OF
THE UNIVERSITY OF PENNSYLVANIA, AND MEMBER
OF SEVERAL LEARNED SOCIETIES.

ACCOMPANIED BY AN ENGRAVING.

PHILADELPHIA:
PUBLISHED BY M. CAREY AND SON,
NO. 126, CHESNUT STREET.

1819.

A NEW THEORY

OF

GALVANISM.

—•◆•—

I HAVE for some time been of opinion that the principle extricated by the Voltaic pile is a compound of caloric and electricity, both being original and collateral products of Galvanic action.

The grounds of this conviction and some recent experiments confirming it, are stated in the following paper.

It is well known that heat is liberated by Voltaic apparatus, in a manner and degree which has not been imitated by means of mechanical electricity; and that the latter, while it strikes at a greater distance, and pervades conductors with much greater speed, can with difficulty be made to effect the slightest decompositions. Wollaston, it is true, decomposed water by means of it; but the experiment was performed of necessity on a scale too minute to permit of his ascertaining, whether there were any divellent polar attractions exercised towards the atoms, as in the case of the pile. The result was probably caused by mechanical concussion, or that process by which the particles of matter are dispersed when a battery is discharged through them. The opinion of Dr.

Thomson, that the fluid of the pile is in quantity greater, in intensity less, than that evolved by the machine, is very inconsistent with the experiments of the chemist above mentioned, who, before he could effect the separation of the elements of water by mechanical electricity, was obliged to confine its emission to a point imperceptible to the naked eye. If already so highly intense, wherefore the necessity of a further concentration? Besides, were the distinction made by Dr. Thomson correct, the more concentrated fluid generated by a Galvanic apparatus of a great many small pairs, ought most to resemble that of the ordinary electricity; but the opposite is the case. The ignition produced by a few large Galvanic plates, where the intensity is of course low, is a result most analogous to the chemical effects of a common electrical battery. According to my view, caloric and electricity may be distinguished by the following chacteristics. The former permeates all matter more or less, though with very different degrees of facility. It radiates through air, with immeasurable celerity, and distributing itself in the interior of bodies, communicates a reciprocally repellent power to atoms but not to masses. Electricity does not radiate in or through any matter; and while it pervades some bodies, as metals, with almost infinite velocity; by others, it is so far from being conducted that it can only pass through them by a fracture or perforation. Distributing itself over surfaces only, it causes repulsion between masses, but not between the particles of the same mass. The disposition of the last mentioned principle to get off by neighbouring conductors, and of the other to combine with the adjoining matter or to escape by radiation, would prevent them from being collected at the positive pole, if not in combination with each other. Were it not for a modification of their properties, consequent to some such union, they could not, in piles of thousands of pairs, be carried forward through the open air and moisture; the one so well calculated to conduct away electricity, the other so favourable to the radiation of caloric.

Pure electricity does not expand the slips of gold leaf, between which it causes repulsion, nor does caloric cause any repulsion in the ignited masses which it expands. But as the compound fluid extricated by Galvanic action, which I shall call electro-caloric, distributes itself through the interior of bodies, and is evidently productive of corpuscular repulsion, it is in this respect more allied to caloric, than to electricity.

It is true, that when common electricity causes the deflagration of metals, as by the discharge of a Leyden jar, it must be supposed to insinuate itself within them, and cause a re-action between their particles. But in this case, agreeably to my hypothesis, the electric fluid combines with the latent caloric previously existing there, and, adding to its repulsive agency, causes it to overpower cohesion.

Sir Humphrey Davy was so much at a loss to account for the continued ignition of wire at the poles of a Voltaic apparatus, that he considers it an objection to the materiality of heat; since the wire could not be imagined to contain sufficient caloric to keep up the emission of this principle for an unlimited time. But if we conceive an accumulation of heat to accompany that of electricity throughout the series; and to be propagated from one end to the other, the explanation of the phenomenon in question is attended by no difficulty.

The effect of the Galvanic fluid on charcoal is very consistent with my views, since, next to metals, it is one of the best conductors of electricity, and the worst of heat, and would therefore arrest the last and allow the other to pass on. Though peculiarly liable to intense ignition when exposed between the poles of the Voltaic apparatus, it seems to me it does not display this characteristic with common electricity. According to Sir Humphey Davy, when in connection with the positive pole, and communicating by a platina wire with the negative pole, the latter is less heated than when, with respect to the poles, the situation of the wire and charcoal is reversed. The rationale is obvious : charcoal, being a bad conductor, and a good radiator, prevents the greater part of the heat from reaching the platina, when placed between it and the source whence the heat flows.

I had observed that as the number of pairs in Volta's pile had been extended, and their size and the energy of interposed agents lessened, the ratio of the electrical effects to those of heat had increased; till in

De Luc's column they had become completely pre-dominant; and, on the other hand, when the pairs were made larger and fewer, (as in Children's apparatus,) the calorific influence had gained the ascendancy. I was led to go farther in this way, and to examine whether one pair of plates of enormous size, or what might be equivalent thereto, would not exhibit heat more purely, and demonstrate it, equally with the electric fluid, a primary product of Galvanic combinations. The elementary battery of Wollaston, though productive of an evanescent ignition, was too minute to allow him to make the observations which I had in view.

Twenty copper and twenty zinc plates, about nineteen inches square, were supported vertically in a frame, the different metals alternating at one half inch distance from each other. All the plates of the same kind of metal were soldered to a common slip, so that each set of homogeneous plates formed one continuous metallic superficies. When the copper and zinc surfaces thus formed, are united by an intervening wire, and the whole immerged in an acid, or aceto-saline solution, in a vessel devoid of partitions, the wire becomes intensely ignited; and when hydrogen is liberated it usually takes fire, producing a very beautiful undulating or corruscating flame.

I am confident, that if Volta and the other investigators of Galvanism, instead of multiplying the pairs of Galvanic plates, had sought to increase the effect by enlarging one pair as I have done, (for I consider the copper and zinc surfaces as reduced to two by the connection) the apparatus would have been considered as presenting a new mode of evolving heat as a primary effect independently of electrical influence. There is no other indication of electricity when wires from the two surfaces touch the tongue, than a slight taste, such as is excited by small pieces of zinc and silver laid on it and under it, and brought into contact with each other.

It was with a view of examining the effects of the proximity and alternation in the heterogeneous plates that I had them cut into separate squares. By having them thus divided, I have been enabled to ascertain that when all of one kind of metal are ranged on one side of the frame, and all of the other kind on the other side of it, the effect is no greater than might be expected from one pair of plates.

Volta, considering the changes consequent to his contrivance as the effect of a movement in the electric fluid, called the process electro-motion, and the plates producing it electro-motors. But the phenomena show that the plates, as I have arranged them, are calori-motors, or heat movers, and the effect calori-motion. That this is a new view of the subject, may be inferred from the following passage in Davy's Elements. 'That great chemist observes, " When very small conducting surfaces are used for conveying very large quantities of electricity, they become ignited; and of the different conductors that have been compared, charcoal is most easily heated by electrical discharges*, next iron, platina, gold, then copper, and lastly zinc. The phenomena of electrical ignition, whether taking place in gaseous, fluid, or solid bodies, always seem to be the result of a violent exertion of the electrical attractive and repellent powers, which may be connected with motions of the particles of the sub-stances affected. That no subtile fluid, such as the matter of heat has been imagined to be, can be discharged from these substances, in consequence of the effect of the electricity, seems probable, from the circumstance, that a wire of platina may be preserved in a state of intense ignition in vacuo, by means of the Voltaic apparatus, for an unlimited time; and such a wire cannot be supposed to contain an inexhaustible quantity of subtile matter."

But I demand where are the repellant and attractive powers to which the ignition produced by the Calorimotor can be attributed? Besides, I would beg leave respectfully to enquire of this illustrious author, whence the necessity of considering the heat evolved under the circumstances alluded to as the effect of the electrical fluid; or why we may not as well suppose the latter to be excited by the heat? It is evident, as he observes, that a wire cannot be supposed to contain an inexhaustible supply of matter however subtilé ; but wherefore may not one

---

* The conclusions are drawn from experiments made by the electricity of the Voltaic apparatus.

B

kind of subtile matter be supplied to it from the apparatus as well as another? Especially, when to suppose such a supply is quite as inconsistent with the characteristics of pure electricity, as with those of pure caloric?

It is evident from Mr. Children's paper in the Annals of Philosophy, on the subject of his large apparatus, that the ignition produced by it was ascribed to electrical excitement.

For the purpose of ascertaining the necessity of the alternation and proximity of the copper and zinc plates, it has been mentioned that distinct square sheets were employed. The experiments have since been repeated and found to succeed by Dr. Patterson and Mr. Lukens, by means of two continuous sheets, one of zinc, the other of copper, wound into two concentric coils or spirals. This, though the circumstance was not known to them, was the form I had myself proposed to adopt, and had suggested as a convenient for a Galvanic apparatus to several friends at the beginning of the winter*; though the consideration above stated induced me to prefer for a first experiment a more manageable arrangement.

Since writing the above I find that when, in the apparatus of twenty copper and twenty zinc plates, ten copper plates on one side, are connected with ten zinc on the other, and a communication made be-

---

* Especially to Dr. T. P. Jones, and Mr. Rubens Peale, who remember the suggestion.

tween the remaining twenty by a piece of iron wire, about the eighth of an inch in diameter, the wire enters into a vivid state of combustion on the immersion of the plates. Platina wire equal to No. 18, (the largest I had at hand) is rapidly fused if substituted for the iron.

This arrangement is equivalent to a battery of two large Galvanic pairs; excepting that there is no insulation, all the plates being plunged in one vessel. I have usually separated the pairs by a board, extending across the frame merely.

Indeed, when the forty plates were successively associated in pairs, of copper and zinc, though suspended in a fluid held in a common recipient without partitions; there was considerable intensity of Galvanic action. This shows that, independently of any power of conducting electricity, there is some movement in the solvent fluid which tends to carry forward the Galvanic principle from the copper to the zinc end of the series. I infer that electro-caloric is communicated in this case by circulation, and that in non-elastic fluids the same difficulty exists as to its retrocession from the positive to the negative end of the series, as is found in the downward passage of caloric through them.

It ought to be mentioned, that the connecting wire should be placed between the heterogeneous surfaces before their immersion, as the most intense ignition takes place immediately afterwards. If the connection be made after the plates are immersed, the effect is much less powerful; and sometimes after two or three immersions the apparatus loses its power, though the action of the solvent should become in the interim much more violent. Without any change in the latter, after the plates have been for some time suspended in the air, they regain their efficacy. I had observed in a Galvanic pile of three hundred pairs of two inches square, a like consequence resulting from a simultaneous immersion of the whole*. The bars holding the plates were balanced by weights, as window sashes are, so that all the plates could be very quickly dipped. A platina wire, No. 18, was fused into a globule, while the evolution of potassium was demonstrated by a rose-coloured flame arising from some potash which had been placed between the poles. The heat however diminished in a few seconds, though the greater extrication of hydrogen from the plates indicated a more intense chemical action.

Agreeably to an observation of Dr. Patterson, electrical excitement may be detected in the apparatus by the condensing electroscope, but this is no more than what Volta observed to be the consequence of the contact of heterogeneous metals.

The thinnest piece of charcoal intercepts the calorific agent, whatever it may be. In order to ascertain this, the inside of a hollow brass cylinder, having the internal diameter two inches, and the outside of another smaller cylinder of the same substance, were

* See Plate. Fig. 3.

made conical and correspondent, so that the greater would contain the less, and leave an interstice of about one-sixteenth of an inch between them. This interstice was filled with wood, by plugging the larger cylinder with this material, and excavating the plug till it would permit the smaller brass cylinder to be driven in. The excavation and the fitting of the cylinders was performed accurately by means of a turning lathe. The wood in the interstice was then charred by exposing the whole covered by sand in a crucible to a red heat. The charcoal, notwithstanding the shrinkage consequent to the fire, was brought into complete contact with the inclosing metallic surfaces by pressing the interior cylinder further into the exterior one.

Thus prepared, the exterior cylinder being made to touch one of the Galvanic surfaces, and a wire brought from the other Galvanic surface into contact with the outside cylinder, was not affected in the least, though the slightest touch of the interior one caused ignition. The contact of the charcoal with the containing metals probably took place throughout a surface of four square inches, and the wire was not much more than the hundredth part of an inch thick, so that unless it were to conduct electricity about forty thousand times better than the charcoal, it ought to have been heated; if the calorific influence of this apparatus result from electrical excitement.

I am led finally to suppose, that the contact of dissimilar metals, when subjected to the action of solvents, causes a movement in caloric as well as in the electric fluid, and that the phenomena of Galvan-ism, the unlimited evolution of heat by friction, the extrication of gaseous matter without the production of cold, might all be explained by supposing a combi-nation between the fluids of heat and electricity. We find scarcely any two kinds of ponderable matter which do not exercise more or less affinity towards each other. Moreover, imponderable particles are supposed highly attractive of ponderable ones. Why then should we not infer the existence of similar af-finities between imponderable particles reciprocally? That a peculiar combination between heat and light exists in the solar beams, is evident from their not imparting warmth to a lens through which they may pass, as do those of our culinary fires.

Under this view of the case, the action of the poles in Galvanic decomposition is one of complex affinity. The particles of compounds are attracted to the dif-ferent wires agreeably to their susceptibilities to the positive and negative attraction, and the caloric leav-ing the electric fluid with which it had been com-bined, unites with them at the moment that their electric state is neutralized.

As an exciting fluid, I have usually employed a solution of one part sulphuric acid, and two parts muriate of soda with seventy of water; but, to my surprise, I have produced nearly a white heat by an alkaline solution barely sensible to the taste.

For the display of the heat effects, the addition of manganese, red lead, or the nitrats, is advantageous.

The rationale is obvious. The oxygen of these substances prevents the liberation of the gaseous hydrogen, which would carry off the caloric. Adding to diluted muriatic acid, while acting on zinc, enough red lead to prevent effervescence, the temperature rose from 70 to 110 Fahrenheit.

The power of the calorimotor is much increased by having the communication between the different sheets formed by very large strips or masses of metal. Observing this, I rendered the sheets of copper shorter by half an inch, for a distance of four inches of their edges, where the communication was to be made between the zinc sheets; and, vice versa, the zinc was made in the same way shorter than the copper sheets where these were to communicate with each other. The edges of the shortened sheets being defended by strips of wood, tin was cast on the intermediate protruding edges of the longer ones, so as to embrace a portion of each equal to about one quarter of an inch by four inches. On one side, the tin was made to run completely across, connecting at the same time ten copper and ten zinc sheets. On the other side, there was an interstice of above a quarter of an inch left between the stratum of tin embracing the copper, and that embracing the zinc plates. On each of the approaching terminations of the connecting tin strata was soldered a kind of forceps; formed of a bent piece of sheet brass, furnished with a screw for pressing the jaws together. The distance between the different forceps was about two inches. The advantage of a very close contact was made very evident by the action of the screws; the relaxation or increase of pressure on the connecting wire by turning them being productive of a correspondent change in the intensity of ignition.

It now remains to state, that by means of iron ignited in this apparatus, a fixed alkali may be decomposed extemporaneously. If a connecting iron wire, while in combustion, be touched by the hydrate of potash, the evolution of potassium is demonstrated by a rose-coloured flame. The alkali may be applied to the wire in small pieces in a flat hook of sheet iron. But the best mode of application is by means of a tray made by doubling a slip of sheet iron at the ends, and leaving a receptacle in the centre, in which the potash may be placed covered with filings. This tray being substituted for the connecting wire, as soon as the immersion of the apparatus causes the metal to burn, the rose-coloured flame appears, and if the residuum left in the sheet iron be afterwards thrown into water, an effervescence sometimes ensues.

I have ascertained that an iron heated to combustion, by a blacksmith's forge fire, will cause the decomposition of the hydrat of potash.

The dimensions of the Calorimotor may be much reduced without proportionably diminishing the effect. I have one of sixty plates within a cubic foot, which burns off No. 16, iron wire. A good workman could get 120 plates of a foot square, within a hollow cube of a size no larger.——But the inflammation of the hydrogen which gives so much splendour to the experiment, can only be exhibited advantageously on a large scale.

C